CONQUERING WORRY AND FEAR

CONQUERING WORRY AND FEAR

GOD'S ANSWER TO WORRY IS GOD HIMSELF

A 10-LESSON BIBLE STUDY

DAVID RUSTAD

Copyright © 2021 David Rustad
All rights reserved

ISBN-13: 9798985086102
Printed in the United States of America

Unless otherwise noted, all scripture quotations are from the Holy Bible, New International Version, NIV, Copyright c 1973, 1978, 1984, 2011 by Biblica, Inc. Used by permission. All rights reserved worldwide.

Table of Contents

Introduction i
Lesson 1: Rest in God's Intimacy 1
Lesson 2: Rejoice in God's Goodness 7
Lesson 3: Depend on God's Presence 13
Lesson 4: Look to God's Provision 19
Lesson 5: See from God's Perspective 24
Lesson 6: Remember God's Rescue 29
Lesson 7: Celebrate God's Compassion 35
Lesson 8: Share God's Mercy 40
Lesson 9: Claim God's Sufficiency 46
Lesson 10: Dwell with God 52
Leader Appendix 57
Bible Studies by the Author 64
About the Author 66
Afterword 67
Acknowledgments 68

Introduction

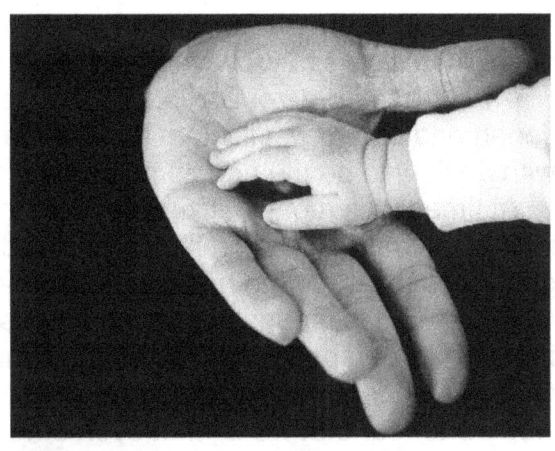

Can God be trusted? That is the real question underlying many of our fears and worries.

Of course, it's easy to trust God when life is trouble free and our hopes and desires are on track. But when difficulties, pain or struggles interrupt, trusting God becomes more challenging.

Because of the presence of sin in the world, bad things do happen. Dreams crumble. Health fails. Finances collapse. Relationships disappoint. Pandemics strike, and more!

Still, God tells us "do not worry," and "do not be afraid." But how?

God does not desire that his children live in a state of fear and apprehension. His counsel to us is refreshingly simple: "TRUST ME," says God. "Trust me with your worries, fears, hurts and pain. I am with you, I love you, and I am always working for your good."

That's a big promise ... but it's also true! In the darkest circumstances of our lives, God is still in control. He is still the author and sustainer of our lives. He remains completely trustworthy, even in times of crisis.

God has a perfect plan for his glory and for our good. This plan is in process every day.

At times, we may not see or understand God's purposes, but even the worst circumstances in our lives do not negate God's eternal goodness, care and plans.

This Bible study—*Conquering Worry and Fear*—is meant to help you understand worry and fear from a biblical perspective. It offers 10 lessons to grow your trust in God.

Through the lives of David, Joshua, Jesus, Paul, Elisha, Peter, Jonah and others, we'll examine how God would have us deal with anxiety to be the people he calls us to be.

At times, this means acknowledging that God knows us intimately and holds us in his arms. At others, it is rejoicing in his goodness (even during nasty circumstances).

At times, this means opening our eyes to see things afresh from God's perspective. At others, it is throwing our worries onto God's shoulders. In all this, God is our rescuer, defeating the worry and fear that we cannot overcome in our own power.

Trusting God is a lifelong journey. We will never completely, and for all time, eliminate worry and fear from our lives. But, as we develop the habit of daily bringing and releasing our worries and fears to God, we will increasingly understand that God fights and wins our battles for us. This is true peace and freedom.

Conquering Worry and Fear is a call to remember whose we are (God's). As we look to God and his unfailing love, we find grace, strength, rest and peace in him, whatever our situation. We can then be confident in this truth: "In all things, God works for the good of those who love him," (Romans 8:28a).

May God fill you with grace, peace and hope as you trust in him to conquer the worries and fears in your life. Soli Deo Gloria (glory to God alone)!

Conquering Worry and Fear

Lesson 1
Rest in God's Intimacy
(Based on Psalm 139:1-18, 23-24)
Personal study: 15 to 20 minutes
Group discussion: 45 to 50 minutes

Worry and fear are often birthed from uncertainty. "What ifs" can easily fill our minds and lead us to anxious thoughts:
- What if I become ill?
- What if my child continues in his or her addiction?
- What if my debt overwhelms me?
- What if God abandons me?

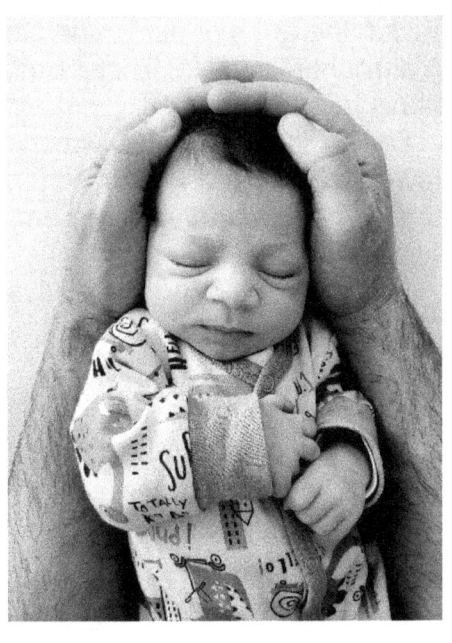

King David, the author of Psalm 139, might not have known these specific concerns, but he certainly experienced various challenges and difficulties in his life.

During his lifetime, David faced persecution from King Saul and attacks from surrounding enemies. He also suffered the death of his infant son, the rape of his daughter, the murder of one son by another son, a coup d'état, and more. Some of this heartache was the result of David's sin; other trials were the result of brokenness in others.

David's life was a mixture of achievement and loss, joy and pain, peace and struggle. Neither David's status as king nor his close relationship with God spared him from struggle and uncertainty.

And yet, David wrote Psalm 139 not about his many troubles but about the indescribable intimacy with which God knew him. God's knowledge of David was complete and perfect, just as is God's knowledge of each of us!

We are completely seen, completely known, and completely held in the arms of our loving God. These truths gave David hope in a trouble-filled life. These truths caused David to love God with all his heart.

David, like each of us, was not a perfect person. He was flawed by sin. And yet, David leaned into God and trusted in God's intimate grace, mercy and goodness. This act can subdue our worry and fear.

Now read what the Bible says about resting in God's holy intimacy.

Read Psalm 139:1-18, 23-24

Q-1. According to David, what does God know about you (Psalm 139:1-4)?

_____

_____

_____

_____

Q-2. Do you find God's intimate knowledge of you comforting, scary or both? Explain.

_____

_____

_____

_____

Note: Some people struggle with God's perfect knowledge, feeling vulnerable and exposed before a holy, perfect God. God sees our sin. God sees our guilt. God sees our shame. We don't measure up to God's standard of sinless perfection. The good news? God restores us to himself in Christ (see Romans 5:8; John 3:16; Ephesians 1:4-7). We can never earn God's favor. We simply receive that gift--God's love and grace--by faith in Jesus, God's son!

Q-3. Read Psalm 139:5. Describe a time when you felt lovingly "held tight" in the arms (hands) of God?

_____

_____

_____

_____

Q-4. Read Psalm 139:6-12. Is God's care for you shown only during favorable circumstances? If not, describe a time when God provided "light" for you in a dark situation?

_____

_____

_____

_____

Q-5. What is true even in those moments when it <u>feels</u> that God is distant (Psalm 139:11-12)?

_____

_____

_____

Q-6. Read Psalm 139:13-15. What does God's intimate knowledge of each detail of your life before birth tell you about God's passion for your welfare in everyday life? See Psalm 139:2, 4.

_____

_____

_____

_____

Q-7. Read Psalm 139:16. How should you feel about the future in light of this truth?

_____

_____

_____

Q-8. Explain the difference between believing that life occurs haphazardly (without order or purpose) versus believing that God uses all things for the good of those who love him (Romans 8:28)? Which do you believe? Why?

_____

_____

_____

Q-9. How does knowing God's word create greater intimacy with God (Psalm 139:17-18)? What steps are you taking to know God? Be specific.

_____
_____
_____
_____

Q-10. Why does the imperfect David ask God to search him and test him (Psalm 139:23-24)? How might you benefit from submitting yourself to God's instruction and correction?

_____
_____
_____
_____

Note: David sinned. He was a distant father. He committed adultery, then attempted a failed cover-up. Finally, he committed murder. He was prideful and disobedient (counting his soldiers when instructed not to). It wasn't David's perfect performance that led God call to him "a man after my own heart," (Acts 13:22). It was David's desire to rest in God's intimacy--his knowledge, his love, his mercy, his character--that caused David to turn from sin and seek to please God.

Q-11. How does God's perfect knowledge of you and the circumstances of your life impact your thinking about worry and fear?

_____
_____
_____

Q-12. Record one important biblical principle (i.e., a promise, command, lesson or truth) you learned from God's word and how you intend to apply it to your life this week. Be specific!

_____

_____

_____

Observation: God's knowledge of his children is deep, wide and perfect. Being intimately known and loved by God brings security to our lives (even when it *feels* like our lives are falling apart).

Key Reminder: God knows us completely AND YET still loves us!

Conquering Worry and Fear

Lesson 2
Rejoice in God's Goodness

(Based on Philippians 4:4-9)
Personal study: 15 to 20 minutes
Group discussion: 45 to 50 minutes

When facing the real (or imagined) troubles of life, the last thing we may feel like doing is rejoicing in God and praying with thanksgiving. That option just runs counter to our natural instincts to "do something."

Still, rejoicing in God is the very thing that shifts our focus from our worries to God's character and goodness.

The Apostle Paul writes about this choice in addressing a problematic feud between two Christians in Philippi named Euodia and Syntche. Paul tells these women to "be of the same mind in the Lord," (Philippians 4:2), before offering important, Spirit-directed counsel about anxiety.

Paul's words? Rejoice. Pray. Give thanks. Focus your mind on what is pleasing to God. Imitate my example.

This counsel sounds simple, but putting these words into practice is difficult. In fact, we don't conquer worry through our own effort. God accomplishes this in us as we lift our focus from our circumstances to his character. God is sovereign, in control and always good. He desires that we cling to him and his promises.

Rejoicing in God acknowledges that God is with us - even in our difficulties. We haven't been abandoned; we are not alone.

Offering prayers and petitions to God in the midst of anxiety-producing circumstances tells God, in effect, "You work this out, Lord. It's in your hands. I'm counting on you!"

This prayer may or may not change our circumstances, but it frees us from the stress of carrying the burden. It releases to God that which only God can carry.

Paul's words still apply: "Do not be anxious about anything, but in every situation, by prayer and petition, with thanksgiving, present your requests to God," (Philippians 4:6 - NIV). When we let go and God takes charge, good things happen!

Now read what the Bible says about rejoicing in the Lord to conquer worry and fear.

Read Philippians 4:4-9

Q-1. Why does Paul command believers to rejoice when he knows that life for believers can be difficult (Philippians 4:4)? What does "rejoicing in the Lord" look like in everyday life for you?

_____

_____

_____

_____

Note: Paul wrote this letter from prison in chains (Philippians 1:13-14), so Paul's rejoicing wasn't circumstance-based.

Q-2. Why rejoice in God? See Psalm 34:8; Matthew 19:17.

_____

_____

_____

_____

Q-3. Excluding possessions and achievements, list four things that you can rejoice in the Lord about today.

_____

_____

_____

_____

Note: It is easy to rejoice in God in favorable circumstances, but God desires that we rejoice in him in all circumstances, even unfavorable ones! This requires that we rejoice in God himself. This rejoicing is relational, not conditional. It is being thankful to God for his love, salvation and presence even when the circumstances in our lives are troubling.

Q-4. Why is gentleness important in our interactions with others (Philippians 4:5)? See Matthew 11:29, Ephesians 4:1-2, Colossians 3:12-13. How might gentleness impact others' worry? Your worry?

_____
_____
_____
_____

Q-5. Is Paul's command, "do not be anxious about anything," genuinely doable (Philippians 4:6a)? Explain.

_____
_____
_____
_____

Note: *Keep in mind that Paul first tells us to "rejoice in the Lord always," (Philippians 4:4). He then offers an alternative to worry in Philippians 4:6. We are continuously confronted by hurdles and impossibilities. But as Jesus reminded his disciples in a conversation about entering the kingdom of God, what is impossible for us is possible for God (Matthew 19:16-26).*

Q-6. What steps are included in Paul's biblical alternative to anxiety (Philippians 4:6b)? Describe a situation where you either followed Paul's counsel or plan to follow Paul's counsel.

_____
_____
_____
_____

Q-7. What are the benefits of bringing our anxious thoughts to God through our prayers and petitions (Philippians 4:7)? Describe a time when God gave you his peace in answer to your prayers.

_____

_____

_____

Q-8. Why does Paul tell us to fill our thoughts with that which is God pleasing (Philippians 4:8)? Is Paul telling us just to "ignore" what is painful and difficult? Explain.

_____

_____

_____

Q-9. How do you apply the counsel of Philippians 4:8 in your daily life?

_____

_____

_____

Q-10. Finally, Paul says "follow my example," (Philippians 4:9). Who is a mentor/role model for your faith? To whom are you serving as a mentor/role model? With whom is God calling you to start a faith-building relationship?

_____

_____

_____

Q-11. It's easier to whine than to rejoice, to complain than to pray, to worry than to give thanks to God. How can you make rejoicing in God's goodness a more consistent practice in your life, especially as it relates to worry?

_____
_____
_____
_____

Q-12. Record one important biblical principle (i.e., a promise, command, lesson or truth) you learned from God's word and how you intend to apply it to your life this week. Be specific!

_____
_____
_____
_____

Observation: Worries (circumstances) that are too big for me are not too big for God.

Key Reminder: Rejoicing in the Lord includes giving to him those challenges that cause us fear. Trust in his character and care.

Conquering Worry and Fear

Lesson 3
Depend on God's Presence
(Based on Joshua 1:1-9)
Personal study: 15 to 20 minutes
Group discussion: 45 to 50 minutes

Ever been chosen for a new role or assignment? It can be intimidating, especially if the task is difficult or unpredictable.

Imagine the thoughts racing through Joshua's mind when God appointed him to succeed Moses as leader of the Israelites.

This was not a two-way conversation. God did all the talking:
You're up, Joshua! I'll give you and my people all the land I promised to Moses. Of course, there are many nations that will fight against you in this process! I'll stay by your side. Be strong. Be courageous. Don't be scared. I'll be with you. You can depend on me! (Joshua 1:1-9 - paraphrased.)

Given the Israelites' history of rebellion against God, this was no small task that God was calling Joshua to perform! Still, Joshua accepted the call. God had spoken, and Joshua would obey.

So how does this relate to worry and fear? Equally important, how does this relate to the challenges in our lives?

Like Joshua, we do and will face opposition, struggles and challenges. Our challenges may not be connected to conquering hostile nations or leading stubborn people, but our struggles are just as real. How do we continue (or even start!) to move forward when our obstacles seem overwhelming?

God's message to us remains the same as his message to Joshua: "Be strong; be courageous; I'll be with you wherever you go."

In God's strength, we can overcome our worries and fears. God may, at times, choose to quickly eliminate the challenges we face. Perhaps more likely, God will walk beside us as we courageously press forward in the face of our struggles.

Why doesn't God fix our every problem in a way that we desire?

It's important to remember that even Jesus didn't have his every desire met by his Father. "'Abba, Father,' he said, 'everything is possible for you. Take this cup from me. Yet, not what I will, but what you will,'" (Mark 14:36).

God is sovereign, holy and perfect. We are not. He works for our good and his glory in all circumstances, even when the good He works is not clear to us in the moment. We must simply trust that his will and his ways are accomplishing his purposes. God owes us no explanation of the "why." It is enough to know that God is with us and will not leave us to fend for ourselves.

Now read what the Bible says about depending on God's presence to conquer worry and fear.

Conquering Worry and Fear

Read Joshua 1:1-9

Q-1. What had taken place prior to God's conversation with Joshua, and what assignment did God give him (Joshua 1:1-4)? See also Deuteronomy 34:5-9.

_____

_____

_____

_____

Q-2. When did you last receive a new assignment or role that was big, scary or worrisome?

_____

_____

_____

_____

Q-3. Name at least three different roles Joshua served. See Exodus 17:8-10, 24:12-18; Numbers 13:1-2, 14:6-9. How might these experiences have helped prepare Joshua for the work God was now calling him to do?

_____

_____

_____

_____

Note: *Natural ability may not be the tool God uses to accomplish his purposes. At times, God uses the abilities he has given us to achieve his will. At other times, he calls us to abandon our strengths so we are completely dependent on him. In either situation, God's presence with us is needed for us to be fruitful for God (see Exodus 33:15-16, John 15:4-5).*

Q-4. How is God using your experiences and abilities for his purposes?

_____

_____

_____

Q-5. What message does God give Joshua about opposition and success (Joshua 1:5a)? About God's presence with us (Joshua 1:5b)? Do these words only apply to Joshua or to all Christians? See Matthew 1:23, Matthew 28:20; 1 John 3:23-24.

_____

_____

_____

Q-6. Joshua's leadership was to result in a blessing to others (Joshua 1:6). How is God using your leadership--with family, co-workers, neighbors, friends--to bless others?

_____

_____

_____

_____

Q-7. Why is obedience to God's word essential in our lives (Joshua 1:7-8)? How does knowing and obeying God's word relate to worry?

_____

_____

_____

Q-8. What three instructions does God give Joshua about his word (Joshua 1:8)? Restate these commands in everyday language.

_____

_____

_____

_____

Q-9. Joshua 1:9 contains a command, a prohibition and a promise. What are they?

_____

_____

_____

_____

Q-10. How is God present with you today? See Romans 8:10-16, 2 Corinthians 1:21-22, 2 Thessalonians 2:13, 1 John 3:23-24.

_____

_____

_____

_____

Q-11. How does God's presence with you, both in this moment and in every moment ahead, affect your thinking about worry? See also Romans 8:28-39.

_____

_____

_____

Q-12. Record one important biblical principle (i.e., a promise, command, lesson or truth) you learned from God's word and how you intend to apply it to your life this week. Be specific!

_____

_____

_____

Observation: Courage comes from God's strength and presence in our lives, not from our own limited abilities.

Key Reminder: God is with us, wherever we go!

Lesson 4
Look to God's Provision
(Based on Matthew 6:25-34)
Personal study: 15 to 20 minutes
Group discussion: 45 to 50 minutes

Worry. It's almost impossible to avoid. After all, we simply cannot fully control all that we would like to control, whether that be health, relationships, money, circumstances or thousands of other

challenges. In these moments, we easily slip into "worry mode," where our negative, what-if thoughts run wild.

Jesus acknowledges this very human response in his teaching recorded in Matthew 6. He reminds us both of who we are and whose we are!

God calls his followers to replace their anxiety with trust in God and in his gracious provision. God is sovereign. He is in control. We can find rest in him.

Jesus also reminds us that our seeking should be focused on God's kingdom and righteousness.

As we begin, ask yourself these questions to reflect on how you manage worry:

- Do I stop to recognize God's goodness and provision when I feel squeezed by worry?
- Do I pause to thank God for his presence even in difficult circumstances?
- Do I thank God, in advance, for the answers he will give, knowing God does hear and answer my prayers?

Now read what the Bible says about trusting in God and looking to his provision to conquer worry and fear.

Read Matthew 6:25-34

Q-1. What command does Jesus give his followers (Matthew 6:25)? What point is Jesus making when comparing the importance of life to food and the importance of the body to clothes?

_____

_____

_____

Q-2. What are those things most likely to stir up worry in your life? Why?

_____

_____

_____

Q-3. What truth is Jesus proclaiming when he references the Father's provision for birds (Matthew 6:26)? How does this apply to you?

_____

_____

_____

Conquering Worry and Fear

Note: God provided manna to the Israelites during their 40-year trek from Egypt to God's promised land (Exodus 16:4, 14-18; Joshua 5:10-12). God's provision is always perfect for our needs.

Q-4. Why do others turn to worry when there is no benefit gained from it (Matthew 6:27)? Why do you?

_____

_____

_____

Q-5. Why does Jesus highlight God's provision of beauty in flowers (Matthew 6:28-30)? How does this apply to your life?

_____

_____

_____

Note: As God himself beautifully clothes the flowers, he also clothes his children in his righteousness through Christ (see 1 Peter 1:18-19, Revelation 5:9-10).

Q-6. How do you balance planning and action with waiting and trusting? Describe a recent experience with this tension.

_____

_____

_____

_____

Q-7. Read Matthew 6:31-32. Who does Jesus say knows about our needs? How is this truth comforting?

_____

_____

_____

_____

Q-8. What, according to Jesus, should be the focus of our energies and attention (Matthew 6:33a)? Rephrase this verse in your own words. How do you practically do this?

_____

_____

_____

_____

Q-9. What are "all these things" (Matthew 6:33b)? How have you seen Jesus' promise fulfilled in your life or in others' lives?

_____

_____

Q-10. Clearly, Christians aren't exempt from troubles, challenges and difficulties (Matthew 6:34). Why does Jesus tell us to focus on the challenges of today instead of the challenges of tomorrow?

_____

_____

_____

Q-11. How does knowing that God both sees your needs and graciously provides for them free you to focus your attention on God's priorities? How does this impact your thinking about worry and fear?

_____

_____

_____

_____

Q-12. Record one important biblical principle (i.e., a promise, command, lesson or truth) you learned from God's word and how you intend to apply it to your life this week. Be specific!

_____

_____

_____

_____

Observation: Worry is a particularly corrosive sin. At its core, it says "I cannot trust you, God; I need to take control because this situation is too big for you." God calls us to trust and not to worry.

Key Reminder: Seeking God's kingdom and his righteous focuses our eyes on God and his provision and priorities - even when we're stressed!

Conquering Worry and Fear

Lesson 5
See from God's Perspective
(Based on 2 Kings 6:8-23)
Personal study: 15 to 20 minutes
Group discussion: 45 to 50 minutes

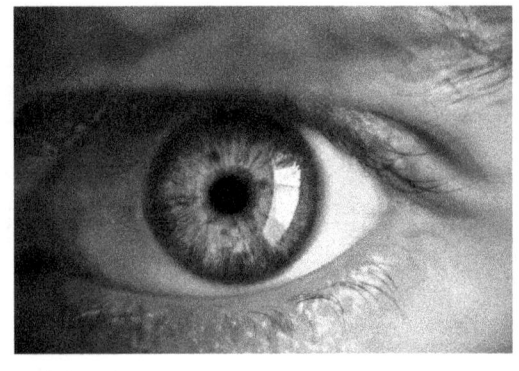

We often lose perspective over those things that worry us. Our mind makes our troubles larger than they actually are. This is especially true when we fail to see God's presence in challenging situations. Elisha's servant experienced this myopia.

King Benhadad of Aram (i.e., Syria) was at war against King Joram of Israel. King Benhadad repeatedly moved his camp to locations he believed ideal to ambush and defeat King Joram. Just as often, King Joram eluded King Benhadad because God's prophet, Elisha, told King Joram to avoid the specific locations where King Benhadad was lying in wait.

Eventually, King Benhadad determined that Elisha was the source of his frustration, so he surrounded the city where Elisha

Conquering Worry and Fear

was staying with soldiers, horses and chariots. When Elisha's servant saw the situation, he panicked! He was certain that only capture (and likely death) would come from this encirclement!

Elisha, however, had a different perspective - God's perspective! He told his servant "Don't be afraid. ... Those who are with us are more than those who are with them," (2 Kings 6:16).

Elisha then prayed that God would open the eyes of the servant. The result? "Then the Lord opened the servant's eyes, and he looked and saw the hills full of horses and chariots of fire all around Elisha," (2 Kings 6:17). Indeed, a heaven-sent army was protecting God's prophet!

Though the servant initially saw only an impossible circumstance, Elisha saw God's perspective and deliverance.

Through faith, Elisha saw beyond the crisis to God's purpose. God was teaching both King Benhadad AND King Joram that Israel's security rested in God himself.

When fearful, we too need to open our eyes to see God's purposes being fulfilled. We, too, need to look for God's presence in every circumstance of life.

Now read what the Bible says about seeing the world through God's perspective to conquer worry and fear.

Read 2 Kings 6:8-23

Q-1. Describe the situation taking place (2 Kings 6:8-12)? How did Elisha, the man of God, intervene?

_____

_____

_____

_____

Q-2. Describe a time when you received or gave godly counsel. What was the situation and what was the result?

_____
_____
_____
_____

Q-3. What did Elisha's servant see, and what was his reaction (2 Kings 6:13-15)? When were you last overwhelmed by an impossible situation? What did you do?

_____
_____
_____
_____

Q-4. What did Elisha say to his servant (2 Kings 6:16-17)? On whom was the prophet's confidence based?

_____
_____
_____

Q-5. Compare and contrast the King of Aram's understanding of power to Elisha's understanding of power (2 Kings 6:8-17). Whose understanding is closer to your own? Why?

_____
_____
_____
_____

Q-6. Why do you think Elisha saw God's deliverance while his servant, initially, did not (2 Kings 6:15-17)?

_____

_____

_____

Q-7. What does God want you to see and understand in times of fear? Are feelings a dependable resource in challenging moments? Why or why not?

_____

_____

_____

Q-8. What was the result of this mercy shown to the Arameans (2 Kings 6:21-23)? How can you better show mercy to others, especially those with whom you have a troublesome relationship?

_____

_____

_____

Q-9. Few of us will likely see heaven-sent horses and chariots of fire. Still, God often intervenes in unexpected ways to protect and care for his children. What steps can you take to more intentionally look for God's presence in difficulties?

_____

_____

Q-10. Read Isaiah 55:7-9 and Jeremiah 29:10-12. What do these passages tell you about God's care for, and faithfulness to, his people in times of trouble?

_____

_____

_____

_____

Q-11. Record one important biblical principle (i.e., a promise, command, lesson or truth) you learned from God's word and how you intend to apply it to your life this week. Be specific!

_____

_____

_____

_____

Observation: "Open eyes" look for God's presence, even in difficult circumstances.

Key Reminder: God is at work, even when we don't see him!

Lesson 6
Remember God's Rescue
(Based on 1 Samuel 17:1-58)
Personal study: 15 to 20 minutes
Group discussion: 45 to 50 minutes

It is perhaps the world's best known underdog story - David versus Goliath! The undefeated, professional big guy versus the ill-equipped little amateur.

At first glance, it doesn't appear to be a fair fight, but David had a rescuer in his corner, and this rescuer made all the difference!

It's true that David the shepherd boy felled Goliath using a sling and a stone. However, the truth of the battle runs much deeper.

David was confident in his abilities, and yes, David had most likely used his sling many times before (funny how God may prepare us for battles using the talents and experiences of our everyday lives).

Still, little David conquered giant Goliath not because of his skill but because of God's sure rescue (1 Samuel 17:37). We, too, can be confident in God's presence and rescue!

Conquering Worry and Fear

When Goliath mocked David's uninspiring presence, David replied, "All those gathered here will know that it is not by sword or spear that the Lord saves; for the battle is the Lord's, and he will give all of you into our hands," (1 Samuel 17:47).

These bold words are truth to which we can hold tight when confronted by our personal Goliaths. God is present with us. God fights for us. God rescues and redeems, even in our darkest moments, always working for our good.

As for Goliath? Well, let's just say things didn't end well for him (it's never a good idea to mock God)!

And David? He did win this battle, though many battles and even tragedies, lay ahead in his life. Despite his personal sin and the brokenness of life, David repeatedly turned (or turned back) to God, the one who was with him and on whom he could trust.

David had a dependable rescuer, as do we. David was not alone in the battles he faced, nor are we. God himself was at David's side, and God is at our side as well!

Now read what the Bible says about remembering God's rescue to conquer worry and fear.

Read 1 Samuel 17:1-58

Q-1. What words describe the reaction of King Saul and his soldiers to the challenge Goliath shouted (1 Samuel 17:1-11)? Have you ever felt similarly shattered, broken and terrified? Explain.

_____

_____

_____

Note: Some scholars say Goliath was 9'-9" tall, his armor weighed 125 lbs., and the tip of his spear was 15 lbs. Barker, Kenneth L., Vannoy, J. Robert (Eds. et. al.) (1995). The NIV Study Bible, 1995, Zondervan Publishing House.

Conquering Worry and Fear

Q-2. As Jesse's youngest son, David served as shepherd to his father's flocks and messenger/delivery boy between his father and his brothers on the battlefield. What did David happen to overhear (1 Samuel 17:12-23)?

___

___

___

___

Q-3. Compare David's reaction to Goliath's challenge to that of the other Israelite solders (1 Samuel 17:24-27). What accounts for the difference?

___

___

___

___

Q-4. Why did Eliab react so harshly to David (1 Samuel 17:28-31)? What distinguishes conceit/wickedness from confidence? Have you ever been hurt by others who questioned your motives? Explain.

___

___

___

___

Q-5. Now put yourself in Eliab's shoes. Have you ever made assumptions about the motives of another without truly understanding his or her thinking? How might you avoid slandering/bearing false testimony against others?

_____
_____
_____

Q-6. What did David volunteer to do (1 Samuel 17:32)? Have you ever "gone into battle" for God? Describe.

_____
_____
_____

Q-7. How did David's past experiences with a lion and a bear help inform his actions (1 Samuel 17:33-37)? Describe a past experience in your life that God has used or is using to help you serve others now.

_____
_____
_____
_____

Q-8. What professional military tools did David reject (1 Samuel 17:38-44)? Why?

_____
_____
_____

Q-9. Why does God sometimes choose to use unorthodox methods to resolve the difficulties we face? See also Judges 7:1-25; 1 Corinthians 1:18-31. Describe a time when God used unusual or unexpected means for your good.

Q-10. Read 1 Samuel 1:45-47. Who was fighting for David? Where is God currently working in your life as your rescuer?

Note: We often narrowly define the outcomes we desire. However, God takes a broad--and eternal--view. For example, God's greatest victory occurred via the cross, which is foolishness to the world. Similarly, God may take us down a path that has little to do with our comfort but everything to do with our growth and trust in him.

Q-11. David, through God, defeated Goliath (1 Samuel 17:48-58). Who deserved credit for this victory? Why is it important to tell others of God's victories? How might this affect our confidence in God's rescue?

Q-12. Record one important biblical principle (i.e., a promise, command, lesson or truth) you learned from God's word and how you intend to apply it to your life this week. Be specific!

_____
_____
_____
_____

Observation: God's rescue is certain!

Key Reminder: The Christian faith does not exempt believers from suffering, pain or death. However, we are eternally reminded that God holds tight to his children in every situation, and ultimately rescues them from sin, death and the devil.

Conquering Worry and Fear

Lesson 7
Celebrate God's Compassion
(Based on 1 Peter 5:7 & Psalm 103:1-17)
Personal study: 15 to 20 minutes
Group discussion: 45 to 50 minutes

Ever been pressed down by a heavy weight? (If you have an older brother, the answer is likely "yes!") You may have found it hard to move (or breathe). In fact, sooner or later the weight becomes unbearable!

Peter may not have been thinking specifically about wrestling, but his God-inspired words to Christians struggling with anxiety are priceless: "Cast it [worry] away; throw it off; give it to God; put it on God's shoulders," (1 Peter 5:7 - paraphrased).

Conquering Worry and Fear

You may be thinking, "Easy for Peter to say! He had no idea of the burdens with which I'm wrestling. They are sticky, persistent and painful! In fact, at times I feel powerless in their presence!"

For some, including Christians, this is the norm. Struggle attaches itself to us, and we just don't know what to do ... except worry.

Peter, himself, knew there is only one sure way to remove the anxiety that holds us. Self-effort isn't enough (we may succeed for a moment, but eventually anxiety grabs hold of us once again). Peter knew we needed to turn to another for help.

Only by giving our anxiety over to God can we move ahead. And we can do so because God himself is not distant or indifferent to his children. He cares for each and every one of us!

The Psalmist beautifully describes why God's people even dare "give over" their burdens to God:

> *[God] forgives all your sins and heals all your diseases, [God] redeems your life from the pit and crowns you with love and compassion, [God] satisfies your desires with good things so that your youth is renewed like the eagle's* (Psalm 103:3-5).

Granted, even this casting away/giving over of our worries and fears to God we do imperfectly. Fortunately for us, however, God deals with his children compassionately.

Worry? It has been defeated by God's tender compassion through Jesus the Christ! God simply calls us to give our worries over to him. And though we may, at times, fail at this task, God himself strengthens us and invites us to return to off-load our burdens.

Now read what the Bible says about celebrating God's compassion to conquer worry and fear.

Read 1 Peter 5:7 & Psalm 103:1-17

Q-1. Read 1 Peter 5:7. What mechanisms do people use today to "throw away" their worry? How long do they last? Describe your coping mechanisms for stress.

_____
_____
_____
_____

Q-2. Do you find it easy or difficult to turn over all of your fears to God (1 Peter 5:7)? Why?

_____
_____
_____
_____

Q-3. List four things that cause you the most worry/anxiety (1 Peter 5:7)? How can you realistically cast each of these worries on the Lord? Be specific.

_____
_____
_____
_____

Q-4. How do you properly balance personal action with trust in God related to troublesome circumstances?

_____
_____
_____

Q-5. What action did God's care and goodness produce in King David (Psalm 103:1-2)? How and when do you offer this response to God?

___

___

___

___

Note: *The Hebrew word transliterated as praise (bārak) comes from the root word "to kneel," and "to bless." It conveys the idea of giving adoration to God.*

Q-6. Name five benefits that result from God's care (Psalm 103:3-5)? Which of these do you most value and why?

___

___

___

___

Q-7. What does the Psalmist tell us about God's very nature (Psalm 103:8)? What does he say about God's treatment of flawed, sinful people (Psalm 103:9-10)? How have you seen or experienced God's kindness in your life?

___

___

___

___

Q-8. Read Psalm 103:11-17. What does God DO with the sin (and worry) we give to him (vs. 12)? How long does God's love and care rest on his children (vs. 17)? How does this truth encourage you?

_____

_____

_____

Q-9. How does God's compassion and love impact your current worries? Of what can you be assured if you've placed your faith in Christ?

_____

_____

_____

Q-10. Record one important biblical principle (i.e., a promise, command, lesson or truth) you learned from God's word and how you intend to apply it to your life this week. Be specific!

_____

_____

Observation: God clearly instructs his people through Peter to throw off their worries and fears. God's compassion for us is greater than our wildest hopes.

Key Reminder: Too often we struggle with our worries instead of casting them upon (giving them over to) God. God calls us to give our burdens to him.

Conquering Worry and Fear

Lesson 8
Share God's Mercy
(Based on Jonah 3:3 - 4:11)
Personal study: 15 to 20 minutes
Group discussion: 45 to 50 minutes

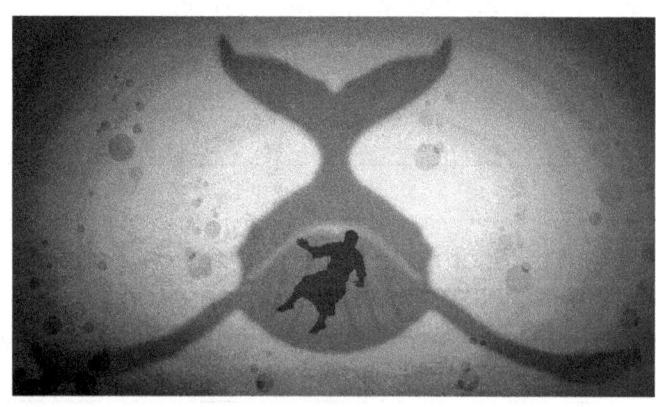

"Life's not fair!" Perhaps you've muttered those words when exasperated by frustrating circumstances: a promotion you coveted that was given to another; financial stress caused by a car breakdown; marital tension caused by the inability to let go of a grievance; news of a parent's terminal disease, etc.

In moments like these, it is easy to believe that even God is "not fair."

Unfortunately, fixating on fairness often leads only to increased worry and anger. Our vision of fairness and justice is distorted by our sin, self-centeredness and biases.

However, God's judgments are always perfect and holy. God is fair and just and good!

God's fairness is best seen in his mercy. Regrettably, the prophet Jonah didn't see things God's way.

Jonah was called by God to deliver a message of judgment to Israel's enemies, the Ninevites.

Jonah was reluctant to fulfill this assignment because Jonah hated the Ninevites, and he feared (worried over) God's kindness. Jonah only wanted to see the Ninevites punished. He cared nothing about their repentance and restoration.

The Assyrians were the folks who had destroyed the Northern Kingdom of Israel. They were noted for their pride, violence, cruelty and for their idolatry.

"Let 'em rot!" likely summed up Jonah's feelings about giving the Ninevites' God's message. Jonah is the poster child for deep-seated ethnic hatred. He lacked any sense of empathy and mercy for the Ninevites.

Following Jonah's experience of being swallowed by a great fish, God called Jonah a second time to go to Nineveh to deliver his message of judgment to the people. This time, Jonah obeyed.

Miraculously, the Ninevites took God's message to heart. They repented of their sin, at least over the short-term. In mercy, God withheld the judgment the Ninevites deserved. This upset Jonah to the extreme.

"How dare you, God?," Jonah lamented. "You are sparing these pagans from the very judgment they deserve. Don't you understand? These are bad people who merit your worst! I want no part in showing them kindness."

What followed was a conversation about, and demonstration of, God's fairness. God used a vine and a worm as an object lesson to teach Jonah about mercy.

Fretting about fairness can and does lead to worry. If you believe there are people in your life who are unworthy of God's mercy ... you are following in Jonah's footsteps. Because of sin, everyone, without exception, is undeserving of God's kindness. Thank God for mercy and grace!

Now read what the Bible says about sharing God's mercy to conquer worry and fear.

Read Jonah 3:3 - 4:11

Q-1. What was the message that God had Jonah convey to the Ninevites (Jonah 3:3-10)? How did the people respond? How did God respond (vs. 10)?

_____
_____
_____
_____

Q-2. Why was Jonah "ticked off" with God (Jonah 4:1-2)? How do you react when you feel that God is not being fair in his dealings with you or others?

_____
_____
_____
_____

Note: Jonah was more interested in vengeance than in seeing the Ninevites turn from their wickedness (God's desire). It's funny how readily Jonah accepted God's mercy for his personal disobedience while holding tightly to that notion that the Ninevites merited only God's punishment.

Q-3. Where have you seen God's mercy extended to you? Describe a time when you wished you would have extended mercy to someone ... but didn't.

_____

_____

_____

_____

Q-4. Read Jonah 4:3. Have you ever been so depressed/worried that you felt like giving up (or dying)? Where did you turn? How was the situation resolved?

_____

_____

_____

_____

Note: The God who created you LOVES you. Because of God's grace, you should be able to discuss challenges, problems and sin openly with trusted brothers and sisters in Christ. Hiding only magnifies our burdens. Similarly, if you are struggling with thoughts of suicide, seek help from a Christian pastor, counselor or doctor. Or...call the National Suicide Prevention Lifeline (800-273-8255). They can walk with you in the journey toward healing.

Q-5. Jonah's anger was not helpful in furthering God's purposes (Jonah 4:4). What issue brings out your anger? Is it furthering or hindering God's work? Why?

_____

_____

_____

Q-6. Read Jonah 4:5-9. Describe Jonah's state of mind. Have you ever bounced from happiness to despair over changing circumstances? How might you better keep God's grace and mercy in mind?

_____
_____
_____
_____

Q-7. What lesson does God teach Jonah through the vine (Jonah 4:10-11)? What does this tell you about God's care for all people (even the ones you may not like!)?

_____
_____
_____
_____

Q-8. How can you stay focused on things that matter, that make a true difference?

_____
_____
_____
_____

Q-9. Has God treated you fairly? Why or why not?

_____
_____
_____

Q-10. Who are the Ninevites in your life, the people you feel "deserve God's worst," or those who you tend to ignore, discount or forget? How does God's message to Jonah affect your thinking about them?

_____
_____
_____
_____

Q-11. God, through Christ, invites all people to share in his mercy. How does God's mercy address worries you have about God's fairness toward you? Toward others?

_____
_____
_____
_____

Q-12. Record one important biblical principle (i.e., a promise, command, lesson or truth) you learned from God's word and how you intend to apply it to your life this week. Be specific!

_____
_____
_____
_____

Observation: At times worry may spill into anger when we believe God is not fair (toward us or toward others). In those moments, remember God is merciful!

Key Reminder: God's fairness is best seen in his mercy.

Lesson 9
Claim God's Sufficiency
(Based on 2 Kings 20:1-11, 2 Corinthians 12:7-10)
Personal study: 15 to 20 minutes
Group discussion: 45 to 50 minutes

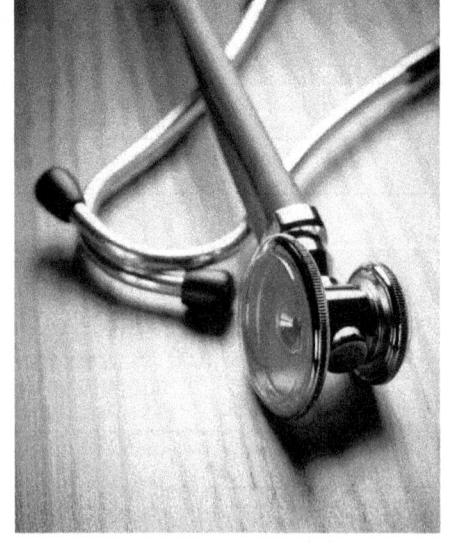

Ever worry about your health? It's a common concern.

The Bible tells us King Hezekiah did, and it's possible the Apostle Paul did as well. Both men were godly (though imperfect) leaders. Both turned to God in their personal crisis. Each received, however, a different answer to his prayers.

In Hezekiah's case, the prophet Isaiah visited him and relayed God's message to "get your house in order, because you are going to die," (2 Kings 20:1). Unwelcome words. Whatever the illness, Hezekiah would not recover.

Hezekiah immediately turned to God--the one who had given him life--in prayer. He didn't specifically ask for healing but to be remembered by God (2 Kings 20:3). God heard Hezekiah, healed him, and added 15 years to his life!

In contrast, the Apostle Paul had what he described as a "thorn in the flesh." The Bible says no more about this thorn. Was it a chronic illness? A harassing spirit? A physical or emotional struggle? We cannot be sure, but we do know that the condition quickly followed a divine event in which Paul was caught up in the ecstasy of paradise (2 Corinthians 12:1-6).

Three times Paul asked that this thorn be removed from him, and God said "no." God told Paul that he was sufficient for the burden Paul would carry. God would use Paul's weakness to show his (God's) strength to others.

At times, God responds to our cries and does heal, perhaps through miracles, doctors or medicine (à la Hezekiah). At other times, God hears our cries but responds "I gotcha! I'll be with you. We'll get through this together - in MY strength," (à la Paul).

When struggling with worry around health concerns, remember that God is sufficient. God sees you. God hears you. God loves you. He walks with you every moment of your life!

Now read what the Bible says about claiming God's sufficiency to conquer worry and fear.

Read 2 Kings 20:1-11, 2 Corinthians 12:7-10

Q-1. What was Isaiah's message to King Hezekiah (2 Kings 20:1)? On whose authority was Isaiah speaking? Were his words a possibility, a probability or a certainty? Explain.

_____
_____
_____
_____

Q-2. King Hezekiah took Isaiah's message to heart (2 Kings 20:2-3) and prayed to God. Why do you think Hezekiah explicitly asked to be remembered instead of healed?

_____

_____

_____

Q-3. Have you ever cried out to God to remember you or a loved one in a health crisis? What was the result?

_____

_____

_____

_____

Note: *While we can be certain that God hears our prayers, not all of our prayers are answered according to our desires. God is sovereign. We can trust him with our future, whatever the path we travel.*

Q-4. Does God answer your prayers based on YOUR merit or goodness (see Psalm 51:1-2; Romans 5:8)? Explain.

_____

_____

_____

Q-5. How did God respond to Hezekiah's prayer (2 Kings 20:4-6)?

_____

_____

_____

Q-6. What was the instrument of Hezekiah's healing (2 Kings 20:7)? What instruments does God use for physical healing today? Describe a time when you benefited from people or medicines God made available in health care.

_____
_____
_____
_____

Q-7. Hezekiah asked for "proof" from Isaiah that God would do as he promised (2 Kings 20:8-11). Under what circumstances are you most apt to seek proof of God's promises?

_____
_____
_____

Note: Whereas Hezekiah prayed and was miraculously healed, the Apostle Paul received a different response when he asked God to remove his "thorn in his flesh." This might have been a physical ailment, or it might have been another type of persistent, nagging burden.

Q-8. Read 2 Corinthians 12:7. Does understanding the why of suffering make it more bearable? Explain your thinking.

_____
_____
_____
_____

Q-9. Describe a time when God ultimately produced good in your life from what most people consider bad.

_____

_____

_____

_____

Q-10. What did Paul do in response to this pain (2 Corinthians 12: 8)? When was the last time that you brought your pain to God? What resulted?

_____

_____

_____

_____

Q-11. How and why did God choose to work through Paul's brokenness (2 Corinthians 12:9-10)? How might you thank God for his enduring presence in the midst of ill health or brokenness?

_____

_____

_____

Q-12. How is God's sufficiency enough for a challenge (physical, emotional, financial, relational, etc.) you are currently facing?

_____

_____

_____

Q-13. Record one important biblical principle (i.e., a promise, command, lesson or truth) you learned from God's word and how you intend to apply it to your life this week. Be specific!

_____
_____
_____
_____

Observation: Healing may not come in our terms or in our timing, but God is with us always.

Key Reminder: Health is knowing the sufficiency of God more than the absence of illness.

Lesson 10
Dwell with God
(Based on Psalm 27:1-14)
Personal study: 15 to 20 minutes
Group discussion: 45 to 50 minutes

Where is your safe place? Where do you feel completely free from the cares, worries and fears of life?

The Psalmist, David, wrote about this place. He described it as a desire to "dwell in the House of the Lord all the days of my life," (Psalm 27:4a).

While David loved worshiping God in his tabernacle (Solomon had not yet built God's temple), the expression "dwelling in God's house" was less about the physical (and portable) tent used for worship than it was about David's relationship with God himself.

David's goal? "To gaze on the beauty of the Lord and to seek him in his temple," (Psalm 27:4b). David contrasts the beauty that is found in God alone with the cares he experienced in the world.

Conquering Worry and Fear

David sets the scene by saying "When the wicked advance against me to devour me," (Psalm 27:2). "Though an army besiege me ... though war break out against me," (Psalm 27:3). Hardly happy settings where life's challenges cannot be found!

David's freedom from fear and worry didn't occur in the absence of trouble; it was present in the very midst of trouble. The very absence of worry and fear that David experienced, in the midst of overwhelming difficulty, can be ours as well.

God doesn't guarantee us the absence of troubles and challenges in this life. Even Jesus had troubles: harassment and hatred from Israel's religious leaders; a betrayer among his disciples; followers who fled him during his arrest; unending demands on his time and attention; even the fulfillment of his Father's purposes came through the cross!

God himself promises to be our stronghold and dwelling (the "place" where we can worship, be in relationship with the Almighty and find peace, rest and strength). Freedom from worry comes through attachment to God in Christ. This place, being in God's presence, can be the center of our desires and life.

Now read what the Bible says about dwelling in the house of the Lord to conquer worry and fear.

Read Psalm 27:1-14

Q-1. Restate Psalm 27:1 in your own words. How do these characteristics of God eliminate the presence of fear?

_____

_____

_____

_____

Conquering Worry and Fear

Q-2. Read Psalm 27:2. What opposition (i.e., person or circumstance) do you currently face?

_____

_____

_____

Q-3. Why do you think David was so confident about the ultimate defeat of his opposition (Psalm 27:3)? What or who is your source of hope when life is difficult?

_____

_____

_____

Q-4. What did David desire of God (Psalm 27:4-5)? What was the result of God's presence and protection for David?

_____

_____

_____

Note: *Solomon's temple had not yet been built when David wrote this psalm.*

Q-5. Describe a recent time when you experienced "dwelling with God." How did God demonstrate his love and care? What happens to worry when we dwell with God?

_____

_____

_____

Q-6. With what attitude did David offer sacrifices to God (Psalm 27:6b)? How might you more joyfully spend time with God?

_____

_____

_____

_____

Q-7. Name at least five things that David requests of God (Psalm 27:7-9). Which of these would you most like to receive from God today? Why?

_____

_____

_____

_____

Q-8. Who is more faithful than even one's mother and father (Psalm 27:10)? What does this tell you about God's faithfulness to you?

_____

_____

_____

_____

Q-9. Read Psalm 27:11-13. Why is it important to know God's ways? Describe an issue in which it feels God is giving you a personal "master class" (i.e., in-depth training in his truth).

_____

_____

_____

_____

Q-10. David's final instruction to others (and himself) is to "wait for the Lord," (Psalm 27:14). What does this mean? How do you practically do this when hard pressed by challenges or worries?

_____

_____

_____

_____

Q-11. Record one important biblical principle (i.e., a promise, command, lesson or truth) you learned from God's word and how you intend to apply it to your life this week. Be specific!

_____

_____

_____

Observation: When the things we count on for stability fall away, remember that God is always present and is our light and salvation.

Key Reminder: Safety is not the absence of difficulties; it's dwelling with God.

Leader Appendix

F or those who are leading or facilitating this *Conquering Worry and Fear* study within a small group, I've included some brief resources to assist in this task. These include:
- Facilitation Guidelines
- Recommended Timeframe for Group Discussion
- Lesson Overviews

Please recognize that these resources are optional. Please use (or ignore) them as you deem appropriate.

Facilitation Guidelines

Below are some general guidelines for leaders to aid your small group discussions:

1. **Keep the big goal in focus.** The goal of this study is to help participants focus on what God is saying to them through his word. There will inevitably be conversational side trips focused on the opinions of experts, hypothetical situations, and/or unrelated topics. When this occurs, gently redirect your group back to God's word, and always seek to let scripture interpret scripture.

2. **Encourage participation by all.** Some people love to talk. Others prefer remaining silent. Draw out the reluctant by communicating the expectation that everyone will answer at least one or two questions during your time together. As for those who may dominate conversations, arrange a separate (and private) post-study conversation reminding them of the

importance of allowing everyone to share. This may mean asking a talker to identify several questions, in advance, that he or she would like to verbally respond to, but then holding back on other questions to allow others to share.

3. **Be welcoming and encouraging.** There is no more valuable activity than spending time in God's word to better know his character, promises and commands. Warmly welcome each participant, regardless of whether they are a Bible rookie, scholar or skeptic. Also, always be encouraging as wrestling with God's truth can, at times, be uncomfortable.

4. **Model transparency but allow for privacy.** Some of the study questions are deeply personal. "How have you experienced ... ?" "Tell of a time when ... ?" It's likely that not everyone in your group will initially feel comfortable sharing their personal stories. That's okay. Encourage participants to share, but do not demand answers to personal questions. If appropriate, share your personal responses (lead by example).

5. **Start and end on time.** Each week make it your practice to both start and end on time. This is fair and courteous to all. Should the original timeframe you agreed upon as a group no longer work for one or more individuals, consider having a separate group conversation to see if the time you've allotted needs to be revised.

6. **Respect each other's privacy.** Make it known that what's said in the group stays in the group. All conversations that take place within the group should be held in confidence UNLESS the individual specifically gives participants personal permission to share his or her news with others.

7. **Don't be the "answer woman/man."** Your task is to facilitate, NOT to provide the group with "right answers." Seek to surface possible answers by asking additional questions, by encouraging additional responses from other participants, and by always pointing participants back to scripture itself. Also remember that it's okay to leave some issues "open." This may lead to additional conversations and future learning.

8. **Watch for nonverbal signals.** At times, group members will convey important messages to you nonverbally. Averted eyes, crossed arms, pressed lips, sullen faces may convey messages of disinterest, boredom, defensiveness, internal struggle, and more. If necessary, help refocus the group by reminding them of your purpose. You might also have private, post-session conversations asking "How are things going?," or "You seemed a bit distracted; is there anything I can do to help you get more from the study?" The goal is to encourage participants in their study of God's word.

9. **Prepare.** Read the lesson (including the Scriptures) and personally answer the questions prior to leading your group in discussion. Ask God to speak to you personally through his word so that you might better know and love him.

10. **Pray.** Though last on this list, this task is the most important thing a facilitator can do. Pray for God's blessing upon each participant. Only God can open eyes. Only God can move hearts. Only God can create faith. Only God can make truth personal and relevant. Ultimately, the success of your group rests NOT in your abilities to facilitate but in God's presence in his word and through his Spirit. Count on him to be with you and to empower you to lead your group effectively.

Recommended Timeframe for Group Discussion (45 to 50 minutes)

- **Settling in (5 minutes).** Greet participants and allow time for them to find their seats. Offer pertinent announcements.
- **Opening prayer (2 minutes).** Thank God for the truth conveyed in his word. Ask him to send his Spirit to be your teacher, and to help each study participant find at least one truth or lesson to "grab hold of" in a practical way in daily life.
- **Study itself (35 minutes).** The opening introduction to the lesson (first page or two) need not be read aloud (most participants will have already read this prior to gathering as a group; some will not have read this intro). Determine in advance if you find it valuable to include this introduction. ALWAYS, however, read aloud the entire biblical text of each lesson before beginning to answer the questions. You can ask for one or more volunteers to read the assigned Bible passage/s. Next, read each lesson question and ask group members to respond and discuss.
- **Closing prayer (3 minutes).** Offer a heartfelt closing prayer, praising God for his sovereignty, thanking him for his truth, inviting him to continue working in the life of each participant, and asking him to bless and protect your group members. Also lift up personal prayer requests if agreed to by group members. If desired, the closing prayer can be rotated among others in the group (but only if others agree, in advance, to do so).

Lesson Overviews

Lesson 1: Rest in God's Intimacy

God knows us intimately, our thoughts, our words, our deeds. He not only knows us, but he walks with us and has ordained (purposed) every moment of our lives. The Psalmist asks God to search him for any anxious thoughts. He likely does this, in part, to demonstrate his integrity to God, but also to ask for God's work in correcting his [the Psalmist's] course, where needed. Our worries and fears are conquered as we rest in God's intimate knowledge and love for us and as we, too, ask God to search us.

Lesson 2: Rejoice in God's Goodness

God is good. That's why Paul tells God's people to rejoice in the Lord ALWAYS (including those situations that we would never choose for ourselves). Paul then calls believers to present their requests to God with thanksgiving. This is giving God the nitty gritty "nastiness" of our lives and telling him to "use even that" for his purposes and our good. This results in a deep peace beyond our understanding. Our worries and fears are conquered as we rejoice in God's goodness.

Lesson 3: Depend on God's Presence

We are not alone. God is with us! Not only is that news comforting, it is the guarantee that makes it possible to forgo worry and fear! Israel's enemies would not be able to stand against Joshua, because God himself was present with Joshua. God's promise to never leave nor forsake Joshua is equally true for believers as well. Worry and fear have no power. Jesus the Christ is with and for us. Our worries and fears are conquered as we depend on God's Spirit and presence with us.

Lesson 4: Look to God's Provision

It's easy to lose focus. We often pay more attention to secondary matters than to the essentials. Jesus himself tells his followers that it is pointless to worry. God is a good and gracious provider. Becoming stressed about secondary issues in life (food; drink; clothing) adds nothing to our lives. Jesus says we ought to focus our attention on "first things" - God's kingdom and God's righteousness. This alone, says Jesus, is worthy of our energies. God will supply all else needed. Our worries and fears are conquered by looking to God's provision and priorities.

Lesson 5: See from God's Perspective

God sees (and knows) all. His perspective is unlimited. God's timing, sovereignty, and purposes are perfect. He is working for our good even when we don't see it, even when our circumstances suggest otherwise. God calls us to trust in him and open our eyes to the good he is accomplishing in our lives. God is trustworthy, and he is present. Our worries and fears are conquered as we make God's perspective our own.

Lesson 6: Remember God's Rescue

God is our sure rescuer. David defeated Goliath not because he got "lucky," but because God fought for him and rescued him (through a sling and a rock). David's confidence came from his past experience with God as a shepherd. David's confidence came not from his military weapons but from God's past deliverance and presence. Similarly, the terrifying worries and fears in our lives are also conquered by God's sure rescue, a rescue that is never too late nor too little.

Lesson 7: Celebrate God's Compassion

God is full of compassion. He doesn't treat us as we deserve, but showers us with his love. God calls us to cast **all** our anxiety on him. This action transfers the burden from our shoulders onto God's shoulders. The result? Instant relief! Instant unburdening. Instant freedom! We are then free to praise God for the many ways he provides and blesses! Our worries and fears are conquered as we celebrate God's compassion.

Lesson 8: Share God's Mercy

At times, we struggle with the idea of fairness, but God is eternally fair and merciful. Like Jonah, we can easily become fixated on "fairness" instead of mercy. This, too, can lead to worry. In fact, no one merits God's mercy. All have fallen short; all are underserving. Thankfully, God showers the unworthy with mercy and grace. We should hold this same attitude toward all people. Our worries and fears are conquered as we share, and share in, God's mercy.

Lesson 9: Claim God's Sufficiency

God is sufficient for our every circumstance (including our health crises). God may respond to our prayers with healing (like Hezekiah), or ... he may choose to leave our burden unaltered (like Paul) to show others that our strength comes from God. In either case, it is God who merits our thanksgiving and praise. His power is sufficient for our struggles. God's purposes and presence are made evident in our weakness. Our worries and fears are conquered by God as we claim God's sufficiency for the whole of our lives.

Lesson 10: Dwell with God

The remedy to our worries and fears is found in dwelling with God. Worship with others plays an important role in our growth in faith. But "dwelling in the house of the Lord" is more than corporate worship; it is spending time with God himself. This involves seeking God, meditating on his character, praising God, looking for God's goodness and waiting on God. Our worries and fears are conquered by God as we dwell with him.

Bible Studies by the Author

Overcoming Busyness

Feel overwhelmed by life's daily responsibilities? Is your life controlled by too many to-dos?

Overcoming Busyness is a 10-lesson Bible study examining how God would have us find our strength and rest in him. It highlights 10 ways we can flourish in the midst of life's demands and responsibilities, such as by receiving and sharing Jesus's welcome, resting in God's goodness (worship), praying for God's will, allowing for holy interruptions, and more!

Whatever the pace (or season) of life, God calls us to give him our busyness so that we can receive the refreshment only he can provide.

How God Defines Success

Most everyone wants to be successful, but what does "success" really mean for a follower of Christ? Most importantly, how does God describe the life he desires for his people?

How God Defines Success is a 10-lesson Bible study examining how God would have his followers live. It highlights 10 traits that God identifies with true success, such as living for his glory, seeking his guidance, submitting to his will, remaining attached to him, and more!

Success is not something <u>we</u> achieve, but rather, it is something that <u>God</u> provides as we trust and obey him.

Conquering Worry and Fear

CONQUERING WORRY AND FEAR
GOD'S ANSWER TO WORRY IS GOD HIMSELF

A 10-LESSON BIBLE STUDY
DAVID RUSTAD

Many people struggle with worry, yet God does not desire that his children live in a state of fear and apprehension. In fact, he clearly tells us "do not worry," and "do not be afraid." But how?

Conquering Worry and Fear is a 10-lesson Bible study exploring how God would have us address worry and grow our trust in him. It offers 10 ways to better lean into God during life's challenges, such as by resting in his intimacy, rejoicing in his goodness, focusing on his provision, claiming his sufficiency, and more!

God walks with us in all circumstances, even the nasty ones! God himself is the answer to our worry and fear.

About the Author

David Rustad is a professional communicator, author and church entrepreneur. He is a follower of Christ who happens to be a lifelong student of the Bible.

Rustad worked in corporate communications, church relations and business development for a Twin Cities-based not-for-profit organization for more than 35 years. He then launched a church survey business to help church leaders better understand the real-life challenges of those they serve.

Through his work surveying church attenders, Rustad discovered that worry, busyness and misguided notions of success are common obstacles in the faith lives of people. He subsequently developed three Bible studies aimed at helping Christians and non-Christians alike recognize that freedom from worry, busyness and misguided striving only comes through trusting in what God in Christ has done and is doing in their lives.

Rustad is active in lay ministry and cares deeply about the spiritual health and growth of God's people. A Minnesota native, he resides in Saint Paul, Minn., with his wife, Lynne.

Afterword

The older I become the more convinced I am that God's love for me does not depend upon either my spotty performance or the circumstances I find myself facing; it relies on God's unchanging character and unfailing promises! This means I have peace by what God has done for me in Christ and continues working in me through his Spirit. This gives me hope and calms my fears!

I do not know the circumstances of your life. I do not know the number or depth of your challenges, but I offer this advice: Cast your cares on God. He is with you (even now), and he is for you!

God will prove himself sufficient in this moment. Lean in. Hold tight. The one who loved you enough to take your sin upon himself on the cross passionately cares for you. Find grace, strength, rest and peace in him! -- Dave

Acknowledgments

First, "thank you" to the many people who have shown me the beauty of Christ in their words and their actions. This is especially true of my wife, Lynne, but also of family, friends, coworkers, fellow Bible study explorers, pastors, teachers and those in my church family. The blessing of your presence in my life (and God's presence through you) is more than words can describe. Know that you are a true gift to me, and I thank God for you!

Many thanks also to those who reviewed and responded to this study: Mark, Megan, Luke, Kaela, Deb, JoAnne, Jim, Joyce, Ken, Connie, Aaron, Amy, Jean, Dave, John and Mark. Thanks, as well, to members of the Emmaus Thursday night Bible study group for your willingness to "test drive" this study! I am grateful for your encouragement and feedback.

Finally, I wish to reiterate here what I said in the Introduction: all glory belongs to God alone. He is ever trustworthy and deserving of our praise! He is the one who conquers all worry and fear!

Photo Credits

Source	Page
Photo by Nathan Cowley from Pexels	Cover
Image by Liane Metzler on Unsplash	i
Photo by Damir Spanic on Unsplash	1
Photo by Bruce Mars on Unsplash	7
Photo by Hu Chen on Unsplash	13
Photo by Elena Taranenko on Unsplash	19
Photo by Victor Freitas on Unsplash	24
Image by Jeff Jacobs from Pixabay	29
Image by Hebi B. from Pixabay	35
Image by Jeff Jacobs from Pixabay	40
Photo by Bill Oxford on Unsplash	46
Photo by Matt Botsford on Unsplash	52

www.ingramcontent.com/pod-product-compliance
Lightning Source LLC
Chambersburg PA
CBHW060420050426
42449CB00009B/2045